CONTENTS

INTRODUCTION

This Pocket Reference Guide is a concise, comprehensive source for information on WordPerfect. It is for the beginning or advanced user who is familiar with how WordPerfect operates but needs either a refresher on exactly what certain commands accomplish or a keystroke-by-keystroke guide. It includes those features added in WordPerfect Version 4.2.

The following conventions are used throughout the Pocket Reference Guide:

- A plus sign between two keystrokes indicates that the keys must be pressed at the same time. For example, CTRL + END means that while holding down the CTRL key you press END and then release both keys.

- A comma between two keystrokes indicates that the keys must be pressed sequentially. For instance, HOME, SPACEBAR means press HOME and release it, and then press the SPACEBAR.

- WordPerfect function key names are listed in CAPITALS, and the keystrokes are provided in parentheses following the name, such as EXIT (F7) or PRINT (SHIFT + F7).

There are three main parts to this reference guide. The first part offers general reminders for successfully using WordPerfect. The second part covers the fast methods of moving the cursor and editing text, and provides a list of the names assigned to each of the function keys; it is the function keys that control access to the majority of the sophisticated features available in WordPerfect. The third part, which comprises the bulk of this reference guide, presents in alphabetical order a list of features giving 1) the sequence of keystrokes to activate a feature, 2) an explanation of that feature's purpose, and 3) the resulting code inserted into the text (not all the features result in a code). Quick answers are easy to find with the WordPerfect Pocket Reference.

GENERAL REMINDERS

Keep the following procedures in mind to work effectively with WordPerfect and to avoid potential problems.

Activating Features and Commands

- After pressing a function key, read WordPerfect's prompts carefully for an indication of what to do next. Any prompt that ends with "(Y/N)" indicates that WordPerfect is waiting for a "Yes" or "No" answer, which you enter by typing Y or N.

- If you inadvertently press the wrong function key and a menu or prompt appears on the screen, press the CANCEL (F1) key to clear the menu or prompt from the Typing screen. You may have to press CANCEL (F1) more than once to completely back out of a menu.

- Be sure to position the cursor before initiating any WordPerfect feature that inserts a hidden code into the text. The code affects a document from that point until the next code of its type occurs in the text or until the end of the document.

Changing a Document's Format

- WordPerfect is preset with default (initial) settings which are assumed for each document you type. These include the following: left margin of 10 and right margin of 74 (for 1-inch side margins), single spacing, 1-inch top and bottom margins, tabs every 5 spaces, 10 pitch, 54 lines of single-spaced text per page. Using the function keys, you can change the default format settings at any time and as many times as desired throughout a document. When you do this, you are inserting hidden codes into the document.

- To abort a format change, you must find and delete the hidden code you inserted. If you know the location of that code, you can delete it on the Typing screen, in the same way you delete text. If you don't know the code's location, you can reveal the hidden codes with the REVEAL CODES (ALT + F3) key or have WordPerfect move to the code by using the Search command.

- Certain of WordPerfect's formatting features take effect at the printer but are not displayed on screen (such as right justification or a font change). Reveal codes to verify that the feature has been activated.

Blocking Text

- When you wish to perform a feature on a specific portion of a text, use the BLOCK (ALT + F4) key and highlight that text before you press the key which invokes that feature.

- With several function keys, a different menu appears with Block on (meaning that you pressed the BLOCK key first) than with Block off. For instance, you activate a different feature if you press BLOCK (ALT + F4) followed by SWITCH (SHIFT + F3) than if you press SWITCH (SHIFT + F3) by itself.

Saving and Retrieving Files

- Before retrieving a new file to the screen, clear the screen using the EXIT (F7) key. Otherwise, you may inadvertently combine files together.

- As you are typing a document, save that file on disk frequently (every 15 minutes or so) to avoid losing hours of work to a power or computer failure. (This can be accomplished automatically by WordPerfect if you activate a startup option.) Be sure to save the file again when the document is complete and before you clear the screen or exit WordPerfect.

- A filename can contain 1 to 8 characters —letters, numbers or symbols (including ! @ # $ % & ( ) - { } ' or '). The filename can also have an optional file extension, which is separated from the filename by a period (.) and can contain 1 to 3 characters.

- Once you have stored an important document on disk, make a second copy of that file on a separate disk. That way, hard disk users will be protected if a hard disk is accidentally formatted or "crashes," meaning that all the documents on the disk are erased. Similarly, floppy disk users will be protected if a floppy disk loses documents due to a mechanical malfunction or is misplaced or ruined.

Printing

- There are two general categories of printing: printing from screen and printing from disk. Printing from screen means that WordPerfect prints out the version of a document displayed on screen, whether or not the document is on disk. Printing from disk means that WordPerfect prints out the version of a document stored on disk, regardless of what is on screen.

- If you try to print a document but the printer doesn't begin, check the Printer Control menu.

Information under the headings "Job Status" and "Message" often provides an indication of the problem.

• If you print a document and the document's format is incorrect, the culprit could be a hidden code you inserted accidentally. Reveal codes to uncover and correct the problem.

Ending a WordPerfect Session

• Always exit WordPerfect properly, using the EXIT (F7) key, before you turn off your computer. This allows the program to close its own temporary files, which are created each time you start up WordPerfect.

CURSOR MOVEMENT, EDITING AND FUNCTION KEYS

Cursor Movement Left and Right

Key Sequence	Cursor Movement
←	One character to the left
→	One character to the right
CTRL + ←	One word to the left
CTRL + →	One word to the right
HOME, ←	Left end of line on screen
HOME, →	Right end of line on screen
HOME, HOME ←	Left end of line (useful if the line is longer than the width of the screen)
HOME, HOME, → or END	Right end of line (useful if the line is longer than the width of the screen)
HOME, HOME, HOME, ←	Left end of line before any codes

Cursor Movement Up and Down

Key Sequence	Cursor Movement
↑ (UP ARROW)	One line up
↓ (DOWN ARROW)	One line down
− or HOME, ↑	Top line on screen (or next screen up if cursor is on the top line)
+ or HOME, ↓	Bottom line on screen (or next screen down if cursor is on the bottom line)
PGUP	Top of previous page
PGDN	Top of next page
HOME, HOME, ↑	Beginning of document
HOME, HOME, ↓	End of document
HOME, HOME, HOME, ↑	Beginning of document before any codes

Cursor Movement with GOTO (CTRL + HOME) in Standard Text

Key Sequence	Cursor Movement
CTRL + HOME, Letter/Symbol	Next occurence of that letter or symbol within the next 2000 characters
CTRL + HOME, ↑	Top of current page
CTRL + HOME, ↓	Bottom of current page
CTRL + HOME, Numeral	Top of page # indicated
CTRL + HOME, CTRL + HOME	Cursor position before last cursor movement command

Cursor Movement with GOTO
(CTRL + HOME) in Text Columns

Key Sequence	Cursor Movement
CTRL + HOME, ←	Previous column
CTRL + HOME, →	Next column
CTRL + HOME, HOME, ←	Leftmost column
CTRL + HOME, HOME, →	Rightmost column
CTRL + HOME, ↑	First line of current column
CTRL + HOME, ↓	Last line of current column

Editing Keys

Key Sequence	Text Deleted
Backspace	Character left of the cursor
DEL	Character at the cursor
CTRL + Backspace	Word at the cursor
HOME, Backspace	Characters left of the cursor to the word boundary (Version 4.2)
HOME, DEL	Characters right of the cursor to the word boundary (Version 4.2)
CTRL + END	Characters right of the cursor to line end (called delete EOL)
CTRL + PGDN	Characters right of the cursor to page end (called Delete EOP)
BLOCK (ALT + F4), DEL or BLOCK (ALT + F4), Backspace	Characters in the highlighted block

Editing Keys continued

Key Sequence	Text Deleted
MOVE (CTRL + F4)	A sentence, paragraph, or page (see also "CUT/ COPY" in the Functions and Features section)
EXIT (F7)	Entire document from the Typing screen (see also "CLEAR SCREEN" in the Functions and Features section)
CANCEL (F1)	Undo a previous deletion (see also "UNDELETE" in the Functions and Features section)

Function Keys

Function Key Name	Key Sequence
BLOCK	ALT + F4
BOLD	F6
CANCEL	F1
CENTER	SHIFT + F6
DATE	SHIFT + F5
EXIT	F7
FLUSH RIGHT	ALT + F6
FOOTNOTE	CTRL + F7
HELP	F3
→INDENT	F4
→INDENT←	SHIFT + F4
LINE FORMAT	SHIFT + F8
LIST FILES	F5
MACRO	ALT + F10
MACRO DEF	CTRL + F10
MARK TEXT	ALT + F5
MATH/COLUMNS	ALT + F7
MERGE CODES	ALT + F9
MERGE E	SHIFT + F9
MERGE R	F9

Function Keys continued

Function Key Name	Key Sequence
MERGE/SORT	CTRL + F9
MOVE	CTRL + F4
PAGE FORMAT	ALT + F8
PRINT	SHIFT + F7
PRINT FORMAT	CTRL + F8
REPLACE	ALT + F2
RETRIEVE	SHIFT + F10
REVEAL CODES	ALT + F3
SAVE	F10
SCREEN	CTRL + F3
→SEARCH	F2
←SEARCH	SHIFT + F2
SHELL	CTRL + F1
SPELL	CTRL + F2
SUPER/SUBSCRIPT	SHIFT + F1
SWITCH *DOCUMENTS*	SHIFT + F3 *2 TOTAL*
TAB ALIGN	CTRL + F6
TEXT IN/OUT	CTRL + F5
THESAURUS	ALT + F1
UNDERLINE	F8

20

BOTTOM OF SCREEN
POS TELLS STATUS ABOUT:
CAPS LOCK
NUM LOCK
BOLD
UNDERLINE
BOLD & UNDERLINE

FUNCTIONS AND FEATURES

▶ Advance

KEY SEQUENCE:
SUPER/SUBSCRIPT (SHIFT + F1) key
6 (Adv Ln)

EXPLANATION: Directs the printer to advance to a specific line number. This is useful for positioning the first line of text on letterhead, or for typing equations.

When WordPerfect prompts "Adv.", type in a specific line number and press ENTER. The text on screen is not affected, but the line indicator (Ln) on the status line indicates the line on which the text will be printed.

CODE INSERTED:
[AdvLn:n]
n = line number

▶ Advance Up/Down

KEY SEQUENCE:
SUPER/SUBSCRIPT (SHIFT + F1) key
4 (Adv Up) or 5 (Adv Dn)

EXPLANATION: Directs the printer to advance up or down one-half line. Useful for equations and other statistical typing.

The text on screen is not affected, but the line indicator (Ln) on the status line indicates the line on which the text will be printed. In addition, a triangle (▲ for advance up, ▼ for advance down) appears on the status line where the feature begins.

CODE INSERTED:
  [Adv▲] or [Adv▼]

Alignment Character

see TAB ALIGN

Append

KEY SEQUENCE:
  BLOCK (ALT + F4) key
  MOVE (CTRL + F4) key
  3 (Append)

EXPLANATION: Attaches the highlighted text to the end of a file currently on disk. When Word-Perfect prompts "Append to:", type in the name of an existing file and press ENTER.

ASCII File

see DOS TEXT FILE

Auto Rewrite

KEY SEQUENCE:
SCREEN (CTRL + F3) key
5 (Auto Rewrite)
Type Y for Yes or N for No

EXPLANATION: Default is on, meaning that
WordPerfect automatically reformats the document after you edit text as soon as you press
DOWN ARROW (↓). The alternative, whereby
you must press DOWN ARROW for each line to
be reformatted, is off. It may be useful to turn off
Auto Rewrite when you are working with features
such as text columns.

When WordPerfect prompts "Auto Rewrite?
(Y/N)" type Y for Yes or N for No.

Binding Width

see PRINT OPTIONS

Block

KEY SEQUENCE:
BLOCK (ALT + F4) key

EXPLANATION: Marks off a portion of a document for use with other features. The cursor must be on the first or last character before you press BLOCK. When you press BLOCK, the message "Block on" flashes on screen. Next, move the cursor to the opposite end of the block using the cursor movement keys or typewriter keys. The text becomes highlighted in reverse video.

The following features can then be used on the blocked text:

APPEND	PRINT
BOLD	PROTECTION
CASE	REPLACE
CONVERSION	
CENTER	SAVE
CUT/COPY	SEARCH
DELETE	SORT
FLUSH RIGHT	SPELL
MARK TEXT	SUPER/SUBSCRIPT
MOVE	UNDERLINE

▶ **Bold**

KEY SEQUENCE:
BOLD (F6) key

EXPLANATION: Produces characters that are boldface (darker than normal) when printed. On screen, the bolded text is brighter (monochrome monitors) or in a different color (color monitors).

When typing text, the BOLD key is a toggle switch: it turns Boldface on if it was off, or vice versa. It can also be used to boldface text that you have already typed if you first turn Block on and highlight the text to be boldfaced before pressing BOLD.

CODE INSERTED:
[B] preceding the boldfaced text
[b] following the boldfaced text

▶ Calculate

see MATH

▶ Cancel

KEY SEQUENCE:
CANCEL (F1) key

EXPLANATION: Has various functions, depending on the status of the screen:

- stops a macro or merge if one is in process
- clears a menu or prompt that is on the screen
- turns the Block feature off if "Block on" is flashing on screen
- activates the Undelete feature (see UNDELETE).

▷ Cancel Print Jobs

see CONTROL PRINT JOBS

▷ Case Conversion

KEY SEQUENCE:
BLOCK (ALT + F4) key
SWITCH (SHIFT + F3) key
1 (Uppercase) or 2 (Lowercase)

EXPLANATION: Switches a highlighted block of
text to all UPPERCASE or to all lowercase letters. (When text is lowercased, the first character
of each sentence remains in uppercase.)

▷ Center

KEY SEQUENCE:
CENTER (SHIFT + F6) key

EXPLANATION: Centers a short line of text
between the left and right margins. Press CEN-
TER before you type the line, or position the
cursor on the beginning of a line already typed.

To center text on a tab stop, press TAB to tab
over to the stop and then press CENTER.

If you first highlight a block of text and then
press CENTER, numerous lines can be centered
all at once.

CODE INSERTED:

[C] preceding the centered line of text
[c] following the centered line of text

▶ Center Page of Text Vertically

KEY SEQUENCE:

PAGE FORMAT (ALT + F8) key
3 (Center Page Top to Bottom)

EXPLANATION: Centers one page of text verti-
cally between the top and the bottom of the page.
Useful to center the text of a title page or a short
letter.

Cursor must be positioned at the very beginning of a page, before any codes, before you press
PAGE FORMAT. The result takes effect only at
the printer, and is not shown on screen.

CODE INSERTED:

[Center Pg]

▶ Clear Document from Screen

KEY SEQUENCE:

EXIT (F7) key
Y to save document or N to clear document
N to remain in WordPerfect

EXPLANATION: Document currently on screen so that you can begin typing a brand new document or retrieve one from disk. (If you wish to use this document again in the future, remember to save the document on disk before clearing it from the screen.)

Colors

KEY SEQUENCE:
SCREEN (CTRL + F3) key
4 (Colors)

EXPLANATION: When using a color monitor, the colors of the background, the foreground, or the underlined or boldface characters can be changed. For black and white graphics monitors, underlined text can be displayed in inverse video or with an underscore.

Columns — Cut/Copy

see CUT/COPY

▶ Columns of Text

DEFINE

KEY SEQUENCE:
MATH/COLUMNS (ALT + F7) key
4 (Column Def)

EXPLANATION: Defines your column layout: the type of columns you desire (newspaper or parallel); the number of columns; and the width within and between columns. Version 4.2 users can select from 2 to 24 columns across the page, while 4.1 users can select from 2 to 5.

CODE INSERTED:
[Col Def:n,l,r,l,r,. . .]
n = number of columns
l = left margin of column
r = right margin of column

TURN ON/OFF

KEY SEQUENCE:
Position cursor forward from a [Col Def:] code
MATH/COLUMNS (ALT + F7) key
3 (Column On/Off)

29

EXPLANATION: Turns Column mode on if it was off, or vice versa. Cursor must be forward from a [Col Def:] code for Column mode to be activated.

CODE INSERTED:
[Col On] or [Col Off]

DISPLAY

KEY SEQUENCE:
MATH/COLUMNS (ALT + F7) key
5 (Column Display)

EXPLANATION: Default is on, meaning that WordPerfect shows side-by-side display of columns. The alternative is off, whereby each column is displayed on a separate page and the screen shows only the column where the cursor is currently located. It may be useful to turn off side by-side display when editing text within columns, speeding up WordPerfect's response time.

When WordPerfect prompts "Display columns side by side? (Y/N)", type Y for Yes or N for No.

▷ Comments

see DOCUMENT COMMENTS
AND SUMMARIES

▶ Conditional End of Page

KEY SEQUENCE:
PAGE FORMAT (ALT + F8) key
9 (Conditional End of Page)

EXPLANATION: Ensures that a block of lines remains undivided by a soft page break. Useful to keep a heading together with its accompanying text, or all lines of a table on the same page.

Position the cursor on the line before the block you wish to keep together. When WordPerfect prompts "Number of lines to keep together =", type in the number of lines and press ENTER. Beginning with the next line, that number of lines will stay on the same page.

CODE INSERTED:
[CndlEOP:n]
n = number of lines

▶ Control Print Jobs

KEY SEQUENCE:
PRINT (SHIFT + F7)
4 (Printer Control)
C, D, G, P, R, or S

EXPLANATION:

C (Cancel Print Job(s): Removes one or all print jobs from the print queue. (Type an asterisk (∗) to cancel all print jobs.)

D (Display All Print Jobs) Displays all print jobs if there are more than can be displayed on the Printer Control screen (3 job maximum).

G (Go [Resume Printing]): Resumes printing after a pause to insert a new print wheel or to hand feed paper, or after S (Stop Printing) has been pressed. To clear print jobs select G (Cancel Print Jobs).

P (Print a Document): Prints a document directly from disk. You can specify which page numbers you wish to print (see PRINT).

R (Rush Print Job): Rearranges the order of print jobs in the print queue, moving a specified job to the top of the list.

S (Stop Printing): Stops the printer (without removing a job from the print queue) until you press G to resume printing or C to cancel the print job.

▶ Convert Files To/From WordPerfect

KEY SEQUENCE:
Exit WordPerfect to DOS (see DOS, EXIT TO or EXIT)
Type: CONVERT

EXPLANATION: Executes the file CONVERT.EXE, a file originally housed on the WordPerfect Learning Disk. This file transfers files from any of the following formats into WordPerfect: Word-Star, MultiMate, Revisable-Form-Text and Final-Form-Text (intermediary for IBM products like DisplayWrite), Navy DIF, MailMerge (WordStar and dBase, among others), Spreadsheet DIF.

Also transfers WordPerfect files into these other formats.

Translates a WordPerfect file into seven-bit or eight-bit format which can be sent over a modem.

▶ Copy Files

KEY SEQUENCE:
LIST FILES (F5) key
ENTER (or type in name of drive/directory and
    press ENTER)
Position cursor on a file
8 (Copy)
Type in name of drive/directory and press ENTER

EXPLANATION: Places a second copy of the file into a new drive/directory. Useful when you wish to back up files as a safety precaution or if you wish to reorganize files on disk.

You can copy two or more files in one command by marking the files you wish to copy with an asterisk before selecting 8 (Copy) (see also MARK FILES).

Copy Text

see CUT/COPY

CTRL/ALT Key Assignments

KEY SEQUENCE:

SCREEN (CTRL + F3) key
3 (Ctrl/Alt keys)

EXPLANATION: Assigns a special symbol not found on the standard computer keyboard to a letter (A through Z) in combination with the CTRL or ALT key. Any key assignment is fixed for every working session thereafter, unless you reassign the key combination.

With the Ctrl/Alt screen activated, press the key to be defined. Then, using the legend at the bottom of the screen, type the decimal value corresponding to the special symbol you are defining and press ENTER. (Not all printers can print the variety of special symbols available.)

▶ Cut/Copy

BLOCK

KEY SEQUENCE:
BLOCK (ALT + F4) key
MOVE (CTRL + F4) key
1 (Cut) or 2 (Copy)
Reposition cursor
MOVE (CTRL + F4) key
5 (Retrieve Text)

EXPLANATION: Moves a highlighted block of any size by cutting it from one location and inserting it in another.

Copies a block of any size by leaving the block at one location and also inserting it in another.

COLUMN

KEY SEQUENCE:
BLOCK (ALT + F4) key
MOVE (CTRL + F4) key
4 (Cut/Copy Column)
1 (Cut) or 2 (Copy) (or 3 [Delete])
Reposition cursor
MOVE (CTRL + F4) key
4 (Retrieve Column)

EXPLANATION: Moves or copies a column of text/numbers which is aligned on a tab stop. Useful when you wish to cut or copy a column from a table.

RECTANGLE

KEY SEQUENCE:
BLOCK (ALT + F4) key
MOVE (CTRL + F4) key
5 (Cut/Copy Rectangle)
1 (Cut) or 2 (Copy) (or 3 [Delete])
Reposition cursor
MOVE (CTRL + F4) key
6 (Retrieve Rectangle)

EXPLANATION: Moves or copies a rectangle of any size, which is defined by the first and last characters in the highlighted block. Useful when you wish to cut or copy a part of a table's column, more than one column at the same time, or part of a line drawing.

SENTENCE, PARAGRAPH, PAGE

KEY SEQUENCE:
MOVE (CTRL + F4) key
1 (Sentence) or 2 (Paragraph) or 3 (Page)
1 (Cut) or 2 (Copy) (or 3 [Delete])
Reposition cursor
MOVE (CTRL + F4) key
5 (Retrieve Text)

EXPLANATION: Moves or copies the following:

- the current sentence that ends with a punctuation mark (period, questionmark or exclamation point) and is followed by a space
- the current paragraph that ends with a hard return code
- the current page that ends with a soft or hard page break code

▶ Date (and Time)

FORMAT

KEY SEQUENCE:
DATE (SHIFT + F5) key
2 (Format)

EXPLANATION: Changes the way the date, the time, or both are displayed when you insert the date (either as text or as a function) for the entire working session or until you again change the date format. The default date format is "Month ##, 19##." Up to 29 characters can be included in the date format.

INSERT FUNCTION

KEY SEQUENCE:
DATE (SHIFT + F5) key
3 (Insert Function)

EXPLANATION: Inserts the date, the time, or both on screen as a hidden code so that the date/time will be updated whenever you retrieve or print that document. Be sure that the computer's clock has been set.

CODE INSERTED:
[Date:n]
n = date format

INSERT TEXT

KEY SEQUENCE:
DATE (SHIFT + F5) key
1 (Insert Text)

EXPLANATION: Inserts the date, the time, or both on screen as text.

Default Drive or Directory, Change

KEY SEQUENCE:
LIST FILES (F5) key
=
Type in name of drive/directory and press ENTER
OR
LIST FILES (F5) key
ENTER
7 (Change directory)
Type in name of drive/directory and press ENTER

EXPLANATION: Changes the default for the drive/ directory WordPerfect is saving files to and retrieving files from. Change stays in effect until you exit WordPerfect or change the default again.

Default Settings, Change

KEY SEQUENCE:
Return to the DOS prompt (see DOS, EXIT TO or EXIT)
Load WordPerfect by typing WP/S

EXPLANATION: Brings up the Set-up menu, from which you can alter WordPerfect's initial settings for how documents should be formatted. Useful if you find yourself changing a default setting the same way for the majority of documents. (See also STARTUP OPTIONS.) But do not alter the Set-up menu to change the format of a single document.

Delete Files

KEY SEQUENCE:
LIST FILES (F5) key
ENTER (or type in name of drive/directory and press ENTER)
Position cursor on a file name
2 (Delete)
Y to confirm

EXPLANATION: Deletes a file from disk. Useful for freeing up room on a disk when you no longer need to store a document.

You can delete two or more files in one command by marking the files you wish to delete with an asterisk before selecting 2, Delete. (See also MARK FILES)

▷ Directories

CREATE

KEY SEQUENCE:
LIST FILES (F5) key
=
Type in name of new directory and press ENTER
Y to confirm
OR
LIST FILES (F5) key
ENTER
7 (Change directory)
Type in name of new directory and press ENTER
Y to confirm

EXPLANATION: Creates a new directory. Most useful for hard disk users who create directories as a way of organizing files on disk.

DELETE

KEY SEQUENCE:
LIST FILES (F5) key
Type in name of drive/directory and press ENTER
Position cursor on directory name
2 (Delete)
Y to confirm

EXPLANATION: Erases a directory from disk. This can only be accomplished when that directory contains no files.

Display Printers and Fonts

KEY SEQUENCE:
PRINT (SHIFT + F7) key
4 (Printer Control)
2 (Display Printers and Fonts)

EXPLANATION: Indicates the set of printer characteristics for the printers you defined: the priner brand and model number, the paper-handling definition, and the character tables for 8 possible fonts.

▷ **Document Comments and Summaries (Version 4.2)**

CREATE

KEY SEQUENCE:
  TEXT IN/OUT (CTRL + F5) key
  A (Create/Edit Summary) or B (Create Comment)

EXPLANATION: Creates a document summary or comment in a double-line box, which is displayed on screen but not printed. A summary is useful when you wish to keep track of the document's author, typist, creation date, and any special comments pertaining to the document. A comment is useful when you wish to insert a reminder for you or someone else who will work with that document on screen.

CODE INSERTED:

  [Smry/Cmnt:t]
  t = text

EDIT

KEY SEQUENCE:
  TEXT IN/OUT (CTRL + F5) key
  A (Create/Edit Summary) or C (Edit Comment)

EXPLANATION: Edits the contents of the summary or comment. For a comment, WordPerfect searches backward for a comment, so position the cursor just forward from the comment you wish to edit before pressing TEXT IN/OUT.

DISPLAY

KEY SEQUENCE:
TEXT IN/OUT (CTRL + F5) key
D (Display Summary and Comments)

EXPLANATION: Allows you to specify whether you wish to display the summary, the comments, or both on screen, or to hide them from view.

▶ DOS, Exit To

KEY SEQUENCE:
SHELL (CTRL + F1)
1 (Go to DOS)

EXPLANATION: Exits temporarily to DOS so that you can type DOS commands as desired. To return to WordPerfect, type EXIT and press ENTER at the DOS prompt. (See EXIT for the method to exit WordPerfect permanently to return to DOS.)

▶ **DOS (ASCII) Text Files**

SAVE AS A DOS TEXT FILE

KEY SEQUENCE:
TEXT IN/OUT (CTRL + F5)
1 (Save)

EXPLANATION: Stores a file on disk as a DOS
(ASCII) text file, stripping it of any special formatting codes so that that file can then be used
from DOS or transferred for use in another software package. Also useful when you wish to save a
DOS batch file to disk. (See also SAVE).

RETRIEVE A DOS TEXT FILE

KEY SEQUENCE:
TEXT IN/OUT (CTRL + F5)
2 (Retrieve) or 3 (Retrieve) (CR/LF becomes [SRt])
OR
LIST FILES (F5) key
Type in name of drive/directory and press ENTER
Position cursor on a file
5 (Text In)

EXPLANATION: Retrieves a DOS (ASCII) text
file to the screen. Useful once a file has been
converted from another software program to a
DOS text file, or if you wish to edit a DOS batch

file already on disk. The key 3 (Retrieve) is available to Version 4.2 users only, and inserts an [SRt] code rather than an [HRt] code at the end of lines that fall within the H-Zone.

Endnotes

see FOOTNOTES/ENDNOTES

Enter

see RETURNS

Escape (Repetition Counter)

KEY SEQUENCE:
ESC
Type number of repetitions
Type character, macroname, or command

EXPLANATION: Repeats a specified number of times either a character, a macro, or the following cursor movement and deletion commands:

UP ARROW	PGUP
DOWN ARROW	PGDN
LEFT ARROW	+ (NUMERIC KEYPAD)
RIGHT ARROW	− (NUMERIC KEYPAD)
CTRL + RIGHT ARROW	DEL
	DELETE EOL
CTRL + LEFT ARROW	CTRL+ BACKSPACE

When WordPerfect prompts "n = 8", type in the number of repetitions. (The default setting is 8 repetitions; if you want 8 repetitions, don't type in a number.) Then type the character, macroname, cursor movement or deletion command.

You can also change the default number of repetitions for a working session by pressing ESC, typing a number, and pressing ENTER.

Exit

KEY SEQUENCE:
EXIT (F7) key
Y to save document or N to clear document
Y to exit WordPerfect

EXPLANATION: Exits you from WordPerfect so that you can load another software package or turn off the computer.

Flush Right

KEY SEQUENCE:
FLUSH RIGHT (ALT + F6)

EXPLANATION: Places a line of text flush against the right margin. Press FLUSH RIGHT before you type the line, or position the cursor on the beginning of a line already typed.

If you first highlight a block of text and then press FLUSH RIGHT, numerous lines can be aligned flush right all at once.

CODE INSERTED:
   [A] preceding the flush right line of text
   [a] following the flush right line of text

Font Change

KEY SEQUENCE:
   PRINT FORMAT (CTRL + F8)
   1 (Pitch and Font)

EXPLANATION: Alters the style of characters (for example, to italics) or specifies a new print wheel (on daisy wheel printers). The default is font 1. On some dot matrix printers, a font change alters the pitch (size), rather than the style, of characters.

CODE INSERTED:
   [Font Change:pn,fn]
   pn = pitch number
   fn = font number

Form Length in Lines

see PAGE LENGTH

▶ Footers

see HEADERS/FOOTERS

▶ Footnotes/Endnotes

CREATE

KEY SEQUENCE:
FOOTNOTE (CTRL + F7)
1 (Create [Footnote]) or 5 (Create Endnote)

EXPLANATION: Inserts a note reference number in the main text. The footnote text appears on the same page as the note reference number, at the bottom of the page. The endnote text appears at the end of the document.

When the note screen appears, type in the text of the note and then press EXIT (F7).

CODE INSERTED:
[Note:End,n;[note#]t] or [Note:Foot,n;[note#]t]
n = note number
t = text of note

EDIT

KEY SEQUENCE:
FOOTNOTE (CTRL + F7)
2 (Edit) [Footnote]) or 6 (Edit Endnote)

EXPLANATION: Enables you to edit a previously-created footnote or endnote. When WordPerfect prompts "Ftn #?" or "Endn #?", type in the note number and press ENTER. The note text appears on screen for editing.

NEW NOTE NUMBER

KEY SEQUENCE:
FOOTNOTE (CTRL + F7)
3 (New #)

EXPLANATION: Renumbers all notes forward from the cursor position.

CODE INSERTED:
[Set Note #:n]
n = note number

OPTIONS

KEY SEQUENCE:
FOOTNOTE (CTRL + F7)
4 (Options)

EXPLANATION: Alters the defaults for note characteristics such as the spacing between notes and the appearance of the note reference numbers in the text and in the note.

CODE INSERTED:
[FtnOpt]

▶ Generate Indexes, Lists, Tables

KEY SEQUENCE (Version 4.2):
MARK TEXT (ALT + F5) key
6 (Other Options)
8 (Generate Tables and Index)
Y to continue

KEY SEQUENCE (Version 4.1):
MARK TEXT (ALT + F5) key
7 (Generate)
Y if no other indexes, lists, tables have been generated previously; N otherwise.

EXPLANATION: Creates lists, tables or an index once you have marked the text and defined the format for the lists, tables or index. (See LISTS, TABLE OF AUTHORITIES, TABLES OF CONTENTS, and INDEXES.)

▷ Hard Page

see PAGE BREAKS

▷ Hard Return

see RETURNS

▷ Hard Space

KEY SEQUENCE:
  HOME
  SPACEBAR

EXPLANATION: Inserts a space which "glues" two words together so that they will not be split up by word wrap. Useful for keeping the text of an address or date on the same line.

CODE INSERTED:
  [ ]

▷ Headers/Footers

KEY SEQUENCE:
  PAGE FORMAT (ALT + F8)
  6 (Headers or Footers)
  select "Type"
  select "Occurrence"

51

EXPLANATION: Inserts standard lines of text at the top of pages (header) or at the bottom of pages (footer). The headers and footers appear on the printed page, but not on the Typing screen.

When the Header/Footer screen appears, type in the text of the header or footer. Pressing CTRL + B within the text of the header or footer inserts the symbol ^B, which is replaced by a page number when the document is printed.

CODE INSERTED:

[Hdr/Ftr:nt,no,t]
nt = number of type
no = number of occurrence
t = partial text

▶ Help

KEY SEQUENCE:

HELP (F3) key
Press function key or type first letter of function you want help with
Choose function from list generated on screen

EXPLANATION: Provides on-line assistance with the functions and features of WordPerfect. Press the SPACEBAR or ENTER key to return to the Typing screen.

▶ Hyphen Character

HARD

KEY SEQUENCE:
HOME
HYPHEN

EXPLANATION: Inserts a hyphen which "glues" two words together so that they will not be split up by word wrap. Useful to serve as a minus sign in an equation or for keeping hyphenated phrases (such as mother-in-law) on the same line.

CODE INSERTED:

–

REGULAR

KEY SEQUENCE:
HYPHEN

EXPLANATION: Inserts a hyphen that will remain between two words. The words may become split by word wrap if they fall at the end of a line.

CODE INSERTED:
[–]

SOFT

KEY SEQUENCE:
CTRL + HYPHEN

EXPLANATION: Inserts a hyphen that will appear only if a word falls at the end of a line in the H-Zone so that it requires hyphenation. Useful if you wish to perform manual hyphenation. The hyphen disappears if you edit the text and the word no longer falls at the end of a line. (See also HYPHENATION)

CODE INSERTED:
— (boldfaced in version 4.2; blinking in version 4.1)

Hyphenation

AUTOMATIC/AIDED (Version 4.2)

KEY SEQUENCE:
Line FORMAT (SHIFT + F8) key
5 (Hyphenation)
4 (Aided) or 5 (Automatic)

EXPLANATION: The default is Aided Hyphenation, where WordPerfect will pause for you to indicate where the hyphen symbol should appear in a word to be hyphenated. Version 4.2 users have the additional option of Automatic Hyphenation, whereby WordPerfect hyphenates most words without pausing for your input.

CANCEL

KEY SEQUENCE:
CANCEL (F1) key

EXPLANATION: When WordPerfect prompts for a hyphenation location, CANCEL positions the whole word on the next line, without hyphenation.

CODE INSERTED:
/ in front of the word(which blinks in Version 4.1)

MANUAL

see HYPHENATION CHARACTER, SOFT

ON/OFF

KEY SEQUENCE:
LINE FORMAT (SHIFT + F8) key
5 (Hyphenation)
1 (On) or 2 (Off)

EXPLANATION: The default is Hyphenation off, whereby words that do not fit within the H-Zone are wrapped down to the next line. With Hyphenation on, as you type words or move the cursor through existing text, WordPerfect checks for hyphenation candidates.

When a word calls for hyphenation, a prompt appears, such as "Position hyphen; Press ESC config-uration".

Move the hyphen with the LEFT and RIGHT ARROW keys and press ESC to insert the hyphen at the location you desire. (WordPerfect hyphenates without prompting for assistance when Hyphenation is set to Auto rather than Aided in Version 4.2.)

CODE INSERTED:
[Hyph On] or [Hyph Off]

SET H-ZONE

KEY SEQUENCE:
LINE FORMAT (SHIFT + F8) key
5 (Hyphenation)
3 (Set H-Zone)

EXPLANATION: Determines the position boundaries within which hyphenation will occur. The default settings are for a left H-Zone boundary of 7 spaces to the left and 0 to the right of the right margin. A narrower H-Zone results in more frequent cause for hyphenation.

CODE INSERTED:
[HZone Set:l,r]
l = left margin of H-Zone
r = right margin of H-Zone

▶ **Indent**

LEFT

KEY SEQUENCE:
→INDENT (F4)

EXPLANATION: Indents all text to the next tab stop, effectively changing the left margin to that tab stop position until an [HRt] or [HPg] code is reached. Useful for indenting a whole paragraph of text.

CODE INSERTED:
[→Indent]

LEFT/RIGHT

KEY SEQUENCE:
→INDENT← (SHIFT + F4)

EXPLANATION: Indents all text from the left to the next tab stop, and all text from the right by an

equal amount, effectively widening both the left
and right margins until an [HRt] or [HPg] code is
reached. Useful for indenting a long quote.

CODE INSERTED:
[→Indent←]

Indexes

DEFINE

KEY SEQUENCE (Version 4.2):
MARK TEXT (ALT + F5) key
6 (Other Options)
5 (Define Index)
Type in the concordance filename (if any) and press
ENTER
Select a numbering style

KEY SEQUENCE (Version 4.1):
MARK TEXT (ALT + F5) key
6 (Define)
8 (Index)
Select a numbering style

EXPLANATION: Defines the location and page
numbering style of the index, which take effect
when index is generated.

CODE INSERTED:
[DefMark:Index,n]
n = format

GENERATE
see GENERATE INDEXES, LISTS, TABLES

MARK TEXT FOR

KEY SEQUENCE (One Word):
Position cursor within word
MARK TEXT (ALT + F5) key
5 (Index)
Type in heading of index entry and press ENTER (or
   press ENTER if same as highlighted word)
Type in subheading and press ENTER (or press
   ENTER if same as highlighted word)

KEY SEQUENCE (More Words):
BLOCK TEXT (ALT + F4) key
MARK TEXT (ALT + F5) key
5 (Index)
Type in heading of index entry and press ENTER (or
   press ENTER if same as highlighted words)
Type in subheading and press ENTER (or press
   ENTER if same as highlighted words)

EXPLANATION: Marks the word or phrase you
   wish to be included in an index when the index is
   generated.

CODE INSERTED:
[Index:h;s]
h = heading
s = subheading

Insert Mode

KEY SEQUENCE:
INS (only necessary if currently in Typeover mode)

EXPLANATION: Characters you type are inserted at the cursor. Existing characters are pushed to the right to make room for the new characters. INS is a toggle, which switches between Insert and Typeover modes. The initial setting is Insert mode.

Justification

KEY SEQUENCE:
PRINT FORMAT (CTRL + F8)
3 (Turn off) or 4 (Turn on)

EXPLANATION: The default is Justification on. Justification on means that extra spaces will be inserted in lines to make the right margin even when the text is printed. Justification off means that the right margin will be ragged when printed.

With Justification on, the printed page will be justified, but the typing screen will show text with a ragged right margin.

CODE INSERTED:
[Rt Just Off] or [Rt Just On]

▶ Line Drawing

KEY SEQUENCE:
SCREEN (CTRL + F3) key
2 (Line Draw)

EXPLANATION: Draws boxes, graphs and other pictures on screen by use of the arrow keys. This feature operates in Typeover mode.

The Line Draw menu includes these options:

- draw with a single line (option 1)

- draw with a double line (option 2)

- draw with an asterisk (option 3)

- change the draw character (option 4)

- erase lines you have drawn (option 5)

- move the cursor without drawing (option 6)

> ## Line Numbering (Version 4.2 only)

KEY SEQUENCE:
PRINT FORMAT (CTRL + F8) key
B (Line Numbering)

EXPLANATION: Inserts line numbers near the left margin when the document is printed. Useful in legal documents or for reference purposes.

The Line Numbering screen includes these options:

- turn numbering off (option 1)

- turn numbering on (option 2)

- decide whether to number blank lines (option 3)

- determine the frequency with which lines are numbered (option 4)

- determine the position for the line numbers (option 5)

- determine whether to restart numbering on each page (option 6)

CODE INSERTED:
[LnNum:On] or [LnNum:Off]

▷ Line Spacing

KEY SEQUENCE:
LINE FORMAT (SHIFT + F8) key
4 (Spacing)

EXPLANATION: Alters the spacing between lines of text. Change to .5 for half spacing, 1 for single spacing, 1.5 for one-and-one-half spacing, 2 for double spacing, and so on.

WordPerfect shows the spacing on screen to the nearest whole number.

CODE INSERTED:
[Spacing Set:n]
n = spacing number

▷ Lines Per Inch

KEY SEQUENCE:
PRINT FORMAT (CTRL + F8) key
2 (Lines per Inch)

EXPLANATION: Default is 6 vertical lines per inch. Can be changed to 8 vertical lines per inch.

CODE INSERTED:
[LPI:n]
n = number of lines per inch

▶ List Files

KEY SEQUENCE:
LIST FILES (F5) key
Type in name of drive/directory and press ENTER

EXPLANATION: Displays a list of files on the drive/directory indicated, along with each file's size, and the date and time that file was last saved to disk. The List Files screen also provides the current date and time, the amount of free disk space, and the size of the document currently on the Typing screen. A menu at the bottom of the List Files screen enables you to manage files on disk. (See also COPY FILES, DEFAULT DRIVE OR DIRECTORY, DELETE FILES, RENAME FILES, DOS TEXT FILES, PRINT, RETRIEVE FILES, LOOK AT FILE CONTENTS, NAME SEARCH, and WORD SEARCH)

▶ Lists

DEFINE

KEY SEQUENCE (Version 4.2):
MARK TEXT (ALT + F5) key
6 (Other Options)
3 (Define List)
Type in list number
Select a numbering style

KEY SEQUENCE (Version 4.1):
MARK TEXT (ALT + F5) key
6 (Define)
Type in list number
Select a numbering style

EXPLANATION: Defines the location and page numbering style of a list to be generated. You can define up to 5 lists in each document.

CODE INSERTED:
[DefMark:List,n]
n = list number

GENERATE

see GENERATE INDEXES, LISTS, TABLES

MARK TEXT FOR

KEY SEQUENCE:
BLOCK TEXT (ALT + F4) key
MARK TEXT (ALT + F5) key
2 (List)
Type in list number

EXPLANATION: Marks the word or phrase you wish to be included in a list when generated.

CODE INSERTED:
  [Mark:List,n]
  [End Mark:List, n]
  n = list number

▶ Lock Files

KEY SEQUENCE (Version 4.2):
  TEXT IN/OUT (CTRL + F5) key
  4 (Save in locked document format)
  Enter password (by typing password and pressing
    ENTER) twice
  Type in filename and press ENTER

KEY SEQUENCE (Version 4.1):
  TEXT IN/OUT (CTRL + F5) key
  3 (Lock and save current document)
  Enter password (by typing password and pressing
    ENTER) twice
  Type in filename and press ENTER

EXPLANATION: Locks a file so that it cannot be
retrieved, looked at, or printed unless its password is entered. Useful for ensuring that a document on disk remains confidential. Make sure to
remember the password or you, too, will be
locked out of the file.

  To unlock a file, use the Block Save feature or
press ENTER when you resave the file and
WordPerfect prompts for a password.

▷ Look at File Contents

KEY SEQUENCE:
LIST FILES (F5) key
Type in name of drive/directory and press ENTER
6 (Look)

EXPLANATION: Shows the contents of a file on disk without disrupting the document currently on the Typing screen. Will display the text but not the WordPerfect format of that file.

▷ Macros

<u>DEFINE</u>

KEY SEQUENCE:
MACRO DEF (CTRL + F10) key
To enter macroname, type ALT + letter, or type 1 to 8 letters and press ENTER
Type sequence of keystrokes that comprises the macro
MACRO DEF (CTRL + F10) key

EXPLANATION: Records a macro, where a macro is a sequence of keystrokes that WordPerfect memorizes and then executes at your command.
Temporary macros are named with one letter or the ENTER key, and are automatically erased when you exit WordPerfect.

Permanent macros are named with the ALT
key plus a letter, or with two or more characters,
and are saved on disk with the extension .MAC.

EXECUTE

KEY SEQUENCE (Named with Characters):
MACRO (ALT + F10) key
Type macroname and press ENTER

KEY SEQUENCE (Named with ALT):
ALT + letter key

EXPLANATION: Invokes either a temporary or a
permanent macro.

◀ ←Margin Release

KEY SEQUENCE:
SHIFT + TAB key

EXPLANATION: Moves the cursor back to the
previous tab stop.If the cursor is at the left margin when SHIFT + TAB is pressed, it moves to
the tab stop left of the left margin.
  Press →INDENT and then SHIFT + TAB to
create a hanging paragraph, where the first line of
of the paragraph begins one tab stop to the left of
the rest of the paragraph lines.

CODE INSERTED:
  [←Mar Rel:n]
  n = number of positions moved

▷ **Margins**

BOTTOM

KEY SEQUENCE: Either change the top margin setting or the page length setting.

EXPLANATION: There is no bottom margin setting. The bottom margin takes whatever is left when you subtract the number of single-spaced text lines and the top margin setting from the form length setting. (See MARGINS, TOP and PAGE LENGTH)

LEFT/RIGHT

KEY SEQUENCE:
  LINE FORMAT (SHIFT + F8) key
  3 (Margins)

EXPLANATION: Default settings are for a left margin of 10 and a right margin of 74. Changes the left or right margin for the document or for a portion of that document.

CODE INSERTED:

[Margin Set,lm,rm]
lm = left margin position
rm = right margin position

TOP

KEY SEQUENCE:

PAGE FORMAT (ALT + F8) key
5 (Top Margin)

EXPLANATION: Default is for 12 half-lines, which means a one-inch top margin. Changes the top margin in increments of one-twelfth of an inch.

CODE INSERTED:

[Top Margin]
n = top margin position in half-lines

▶ Mark Files

KEY SEQUENCE:

LIST FILES (F5) key
Type in name of drive/directory and press ENTER
Position cursor on a filename
Type asterisk (*)

EXPLANATION: By marking specific files with an asterisk on the List Files screen, you can narrow the list of files for deleting, printing, copying or performing a word search.

On the List Files screen, the asterisk is a toggle switch; it marks or unmarks a file. You can mark all files, if none are marked, by pressing MARK TEXT (ALT + F5). If some files are marked, press MARK TEXT (ALT + F5) to unmark all files.

Math

CALCULATE

KEY SEQUENCE:
MATH/COLUMNS (ALT + F7) key
2 (Calculate)

EXPLANATION: Calculates the results wherever a Math operator is placed in the math columns. You can only calculate within the text where Math has been turned on.

DEFINE

KEY SEQUENCE:
MATH/COLUMNS (ALT + F7) key
2 (Math Def)

EXPLANATION: Defines your math column layout:

- the type of columns (numeric, total, text, or calculation)

- how negative numbers are displayed

- the number of digits to the right of the decimal on calculated results

- the formulas for special calculations

You can define columns only when Math is off.

For a calculation column, you must define a math formula, using the following symbols when writing the formula:

+ addition
− subtraction
* multiplication
/ division

Or insert the following special formulas on their own:

+   add all numeric columns
+/ average of all numeric columns
=   add all total columns
=/ average of all total columns

CODE INSERTED:
[Math Def]

OPERATORS

KEY SEQUENCE:
Press TAB until cursor is at correct tab stop
Type in a Math operator

EXPLANATION: Insert the correct Math operator, depending on the calculation you desire, including:

+ subtotal
= total
* grand total
t in front of a known subtotal
T in front of a known total

If a math column has been defined as a calculation column, then WordPerfect automatically inserts an exclamation (!) as a Math operator as soon as you tab over to that column.

TURN ON/OFF

KEY SEQUENCE:
MATH/COLUMNS (ALT + F7) key
1 (Math On) or 1 (Math Off)

EXPLANATION: Turns on the Math feature when off, and vice versa.

CODE INSERTED:
[Math On] or [Math Off]

▶ Merge

EXECUTE

KEY SEQUENCE:
MERGE/SORT (CTRL + F9) key
1 (Merge)
Type in primary document filename and press ENTER
Type in secondary document filename and press ENTER

EXPLANATION: Initiates a merge process, whereby the contents a secondary file (such as names, dates, addresses) are inserted at specified places in primary file. Useful for such purposes as mailings of form letters and invoices.

   If you are merging from the keyboard rather than a secondary file, simply press ENTER without specifying a secondary filename.

INSERT MERGE CODES

KEY SEQUENCE:
MERGE CODES (ALT + F9) key
Type a letter to insert that merge code

EXPLANATION: Inserts a merge code into a primary or secondary document. These codes are:

$^\wedge$C	input from the console (keyboard)
$^\wedge$D	insert the current date during the merge
$^\wedge$Fn$^\wedge$	insert the contents of field number n into this location during the merge
$^\wedge$G$^\wedge$G	go to (execute) a macro when the merge ends
$^\wedge$N	continue the merge with the next record
$^\wedge$O$^\wedge$O	output a message to the screen during a merge
$^\wedge$P$^\wedge$P	continue the merge with the specified primary file
$^\wedge$Q	quit the merge
$^\wedge$S$^\wedge$S	continue the merge with the specified secondary file
$^\wedge$T	type (print) directly to the printer
$^\wedge$U	update the screen to show the current status of the merge
$^\wedge$V$^\wedge$V	insert merge codes into the merged text without acting upon them

MERGE E

KEY SEQUENCE:
MERGE E (SHIFT + F9) key

EXPLANATION: Inserts a ^E code followed by a hard return. This merge code signifies the end of a record in a secondary merge file.

MERGE R

KEY SEQUENCE:
MERGE R (F9) key

EXPLANATION: Inserts a ^R code followed by a hard return. This merge code signifies the end of a field in a secondary merge file.

Move Text

see CUT/COPY

Name Search

KEY SEQUENCE:
LIST FILES (F5) key
Type in name of drive/directory and press ENTER
Type first letters of filename

EXPLANATION: On the List Files screen, moves the cursor to the filename that begins with the letters typed.

▶ New Page Number

KEY SEQUENCE:
PAGE FORMAT (ALT + F8) key
2 (New Page Number)

EXPLANATION: Renumbers pages. You can specify Arabic style (1,2,3...) or lower case Roman
numerals (i, ii, iii...).The status line reflects the
new page number. Roman numerals are shown
only on the printed page and not on the status
line.

CODE INSERTED:
[Pg#:n]
n = page number

▶ Number of Copies (when printed)

see PRINT OPTIONS

▶ Number of Single-Spaced Text Lines

see PAGE LENGTH

▶ Outlines

DEFINE OUTLINE/PARAGRAPH NUMBERING

KEY SEQUENCE (Version 4.2):
MARK TEXT (ALT + F5) key
6 (Other Options)
1 (Define Outline/Paragraph Numbering)
Select a numbering style
Select starting paragraph number

KEY SEQUENCE (Version 4.1):
MARK TEXT (ALT + F5) key
6 (Define)
7 (Outline/Paragraph Numbering)
Select a numbering style

EXPLANATION: The default is Outline Numbering style, where the levels are:

I., A., 1., a., (1), (a), i)

Changes to Paragraph Numbering, Legal Numbering style, or a style of your own design.

For a separate outline in the same document, retain Outline Numbering but restart at number I.

CODE INSERTED:
[Par#Def]

TURN ON/OFF

KEY SEQUENCE:
MARK TEXT (ALT + F5) key
1 (Outline)

EXPLANATION: Switches in or out of Outline mode. In Outline mode, certain keys operate as follows to create outlines:

Enter: Inserts a hard return and a level 1 outline number.

Tab: Moves the outline number to the next tab stop and changes the outline number to the next level.

←Margin Release: Moves the outline number to the previous tab stop and changes the outline number to the previous level.

→Indent: Locks the outline number in place and indents the text you type following the outline number to the next tab stop. (Use the SPACE BAR if you don't wish to indent the text following the outline number.)

CODE INSERTED:
[Par#:Auto] wherever an outline number is inserted

▶ Overstrike

KEY SEQUENCE:
Type first character
SUPER/SUBSCRIPT (SHIFT + F1) key
3 (Overstrike)
Type second character

EXPLANATION: Prints two characters in the same position. Useful to create special characters such as $\neq$ or ė. The result appears on the printed page; the Typing screen shows the second character.

CODE INSERTED:
[Ovrstk] between the two characters

▶ Page Breaks

HARD

KEY SEQUENCE:
CTRL + ENTER

EXPLANATION: Starts the cursor at the top of a new page. Useful when you wish to end a short page of text. Also used to end a column and start a new one when working in text columns.

A page bar (a line of equal signs in version 4.2; a

line of dashes in version 4.1) across the screen indicates the page break. The status line reflects the change in page number.

CODE INSERTED:
[HPg]

SOFT

KEY SEQUENCE: None (performed by Word-Perfect)

EXPLANATION: Starts the cursor at the top of a new page after you type a certain number of lines as defined by the setting for the number of single-spaced text lines (see also PAGE LENGTH). A page bar (a line of dashes) across the screen indicates the page break. The status line reflects the change in page number. This page bar will readjust if text is later edited.

CODE INSERTED:
[SPg]

Page Length

KEY SEQUENCE:
PAGE FORMAT (ALT + F8) key
4 (Page Length)

EXPLANATION: Changes either or both of the following settings:

Form length in lines: The length of paper that the document will be printed on. The default is 66 lines, for a standard page 11 inches long.

Number of single-spaced text lines: The number of lines to be printed on each page. The default is 54 lines, for one-inch top and bottom margins (assuming 6 lines per inch and a top margin of 12 half-lines).

Choices are standard letter size of 8 1/2 by 11 (option 1, the default), standard legal size of 8 1/2 by 14 (option 2) or any other setting of your design (option 3).

CODE INSERTED:
[Pg Lnth:fn,tn]
fn = form length number
tn = text lines number

Page Number Column Position

KEY SEQUENCE:
PAGE FORMAT (ALT + F8) key
7 (Page Number Column Position)

EXPLANATION: Changes the location of the column positions for left, right and center page numbers. The default settings are left = 10, center = 42, and right = 74. Enter the column positions assuming 10-pitch (10 characters printed per inch). Then select a page number position (see PAGE NUMBER POSITION).

CODE INSERTED:

[Pg#Col:l,c,r]
l = left column position
c = center
r = right

Page Number Position

KEY SEQUENCE:

PAGE FORMAT (ALT + F8) key
1 (Page Number Position)

EXPLANATION: Activates page numbering, and selects where on the page the page numbers will be printed. There are 9 options to choose from:

- no page numbers
- top left, top center, or top right of every page
- top alternating left and right
- bottom left, bottom center, or bottom right of every page
- bottom alternating left and right

CODE INSERTED:

[PosPg#:n]

n = page numbering option selected

▶ Paragraph Numbers

DEFINE OUTLINE/PARAGRAPH NUMBERING

see OUTLINES

INSERT PARAGRAPH NUMBER

KEY SEQUENCE:

MARK TEXT (ALT + F5) key

2 (Para #)

EXPLANATION: Inserts a paragraph number at the current cursor location. You can set an automatic number, where the paragraph level is determined by the location of the cursor (automatic); simply press ENTER.

Or you can specify the paragraph level you desire by typing in the level and pressing ENTER.

CODE INSERTED:

[Par#:Auto] wherever an automatic paragraph number is inserted

[Par#:n] wherever a level is specified

n = paragraph level

▶ Password Protection

see LOCK FILES

▶ Pitch Change

KEY SEQUENCE:
PRINT FORMAT (CTRL + F8)
1 (Pitch and Font)

EXPLANATION: Alters the width of spaces between characters. The default is 10-pitch (10 characters printed per inch). The larger the pitch, the narrower or closer together are the characters. Each printer supports only certain pitch changes.

CODE INSERTED:
[Font Change:pn,fn]
pn = pitch number
fn = font number

▶ Preview (Version 4.2)

KEY SEQUENCE:
PRINT (SHIFT + F7) key
6 (Preview)
1 (Document) or 2 (Page)

EXPLANATION: Shows what the page will look like when printed. Features such as justification, headers, footers, page numbering, line numbering, and margins are shown. Certain other features, such as pitch and font changes, are not shown.

▶ Print

BLOCK FROM SCREEN

KEY SEQUENCE:
BLOCK (ALT + F4) key
PRINT (SHIFT + F7) key
Y to confirm

EXPLANATION: Prints a highlighted block from the screen. Useful if you wish to print only a portion of a document currently on screen, such as two paragraphs.

DOCUMENT FROM DISK, Specified Number of Pages

KEY SEQUENCE:
PRINT (SHIFT + F7) key
4 (Printer Control)
P (Print a Document)
Type in filename and press ENTER
Type in page numbers and press ENTER

EXPLANATION: Prints any number of pages of a document from disk.

Version 4.2 users can specify a range of consecutive pages using a hyphen (such as 4-8), or nonconsecutive pages using a comma (such as 1,4,9).

Version 4.1 users can specify a range of consecutive pages by entering, at the prompts, a starting page and ending page.

To print all pages of the document, simply press ENTER when page numbers are requested.

DOCUMENT FROM DISK, All Pages

KEY SEQUENCE:
LIST FILES (F5) key
Type in name of drive/directory and press ENTER
Position cursor on a filename
4 (Print)

EXPLANATION: Prints from disk the file that the cursor is highlighting. Assumes that you wish to print all pages of the file.

You can print two or more files in one command by marking the files you wish to print with an asterisk before selecting 4 (Print). (See also MARK FILES.)

FULL TEXT FROM SCREEN

KEY SEQUENCE:
PRINT (SHIFT + F7) key
1 (Full Text)

EXPLANATION: Prints all pages of the document currently on screen.

PAGE FROM SCREEN

KEY SEQUENCE:
PRINT (SHIFT + F7) key
2 (Page)

EXPLANATION: Prints the page on screen where the cursor is currently located.

▶ Print Options

BINDING WIDTH

KEY SEQUENCE (Current Print Job):
PRINT (SHIFT + F7) key
3 (Options)
3 (Binding Width)

KEY SEQUENCE (Working Session):

- PRINT (SHIFT + F7) key
- 4 (Printer Control)
- 1 (Select Print Options)
- 3 (Binding Width)

EXPLANATION: Sets an extra wide margin on alternate pages for a document that you plan to bind like a book. The default setting is 0 binding width. The width you specify is measured in tenths of an inch.

Depending on the key sequence you press, the binding width stays in effect either for only the document you are currently printing or for all print jobs during your working session, until you exit WordPerfect or change the binding width again.

NUMBER OF COPIES

KEY SEQUENCE (Current Print Job):

PRINT (SHIFT + F7) key
3 (Options)
2 (Number of Copies)

KEY SEQUENCE (Working Session):

PRINT (SHIFT + F7) key
4 (Printer Control)
1 (Select Print Options)
2 (Number of Copies)

EXPLANATION: Sets the number of copies to print. The default is one copy.

Depending on the sequence of keystrokes, this number of copies selection stays in effect either for only the current print job or for all print jobs until you exit WordPerfect or again change the number of copies.

PRINTER NUMBER

KEY SEQUENCE (Current Print Job):
PRINT (SHIFT + F7) key
3 (Options)
1 (Printer Number)

KEY SEQUENCE (Working Session):
PRINT (SHIFT + F7) key
4 (Printer Control)
1 (Select Print Options)
1 (Printer Number)

EXPLANATION: Determines which printer will print the job. The default is printer 1, which is defined when printers were selected (see PRINTERS, SELECT). (See DISPLAY PRINTERS AND FONTS to see which brand of printer corresponds to which printer number you selected for the WordPerfect program you are using.)

Depending on the sequence of keystrokes you

press, the printer you specify will either print only the current job or print all print jobs until you exit WordPerfect or select a new printer number.

Printer Commands

KEY SEQUENCE:
PRINT FORMAT (CTRL + F8) key
A (Insert Printer Command)

EXPLANATION: Inserts a hidden printer code into the text so that you can control special features of your printer. The commands are usually entered in decimal ASCII, as provided in the printer manual. Decimal codes less than 32 and greater than 126 must be entered in angle brackets, such as <15>.

CODE INSERTED:
[Cmnd:c]
c = printer command

Printer Control

see CONTROL PRINT JOBS

Printer Number

see PRINT OPTIONS

▶ Printers, Display

see DISPLAY PRINTERS AND FONTS

▶ Printers, Select

KEY SEQUENCE:
PRINT (SHIFT + F7) key
4 (Printer Control)
3 (Select Printers)

EXPLANATION: Defines characteristics of printers 1 through 6. Each set of characteristics includes printer definition (brand name and printer number), paper handling option (single sheets, continuous, or sheet feeder), and printer port (whether serial or parallel port and which port number). WordPerfect assumes you wish to send print jobs to printer 1 unless you change the print option (see PRINT OPTIONS).

▶ Proportional Spacing

KEY SEQUENCE:
PRINT FORMAT (CTRL + F8)
1 (Pitch and Font)

92

EXPLANATION: The default is mono-spacing, rather than proportional spacing. Proportional spacing alters the spacing of characters so that each character occupies an amount of space proportional to its width.

Change the pitch setting, inserting an asterisk (for example, 13∗). Also change the font setting to one that corresponds to proportional spacing for your printer. Only certain printers and print wheels support proportional spacing.

CODE INSERTED:
[Font Change:pn∗,fn]
pn = pitch number
fn = font number

▶ Protection, Block

KEY SEQUENCE:
BLOCK (ALT + F4) key
PAGE FORMAT (ALT + F8) key
Y to confirm

EXPLANATION: Ensures that a block of text is not divided by a soft page break. Useful to keep a heading together with its accompanying text, or all lines of a table on the same page.

Inserted automatically when you are typing in parallel columns, to keep the parallel columns together.

CODE INSERTED:
[BlockPro:On] preceding the protected text
[BlockPro:Off] following the protected text

Rectangles, Cut/Copy

see CUT/COPY

Redline

KEY SEQUENCE:
MARK TEXT (ALT + F5) key
3 (Redline)

EXPLANATION: Marks lines of text added since the last draft of a document. When that text is printed, a vertical bar (or another symbol) appears in the left margin next to each line of redlined text.

Redline is a toggle switch; it turns Redline on if it was off, or vice versa. It can also be used to redline text that you have already typed if you first turn Block on and highlight the text to be redlined. (See also REMOVE REDLINE AND STRIKEOUT)

94

CODE INSERTED:
[RedLn] preceding the text
[r] following the text

▶ Remove Redline and Strikeout

KEY SEQUENCE (Version 4.2):
MARK TEXT (ALT + F5) key
6 (Other Options)
7 (Remove)
Y to confirm

KEY SEQUENCE (Version 4.1):
MARK TEXT (ALT + F5) key
4 (Remove)
Y to confirm

EXPLANATION: Removes all the redline markings and all the strikeout text from the entire document in one command (see STRIKEOUT).

▶ Rename Files

KEY SEQUENCE:
LIST FILES (F5) key
Type in name of drive/directory and press ENTER
Position cursor on a filename
3 (Rename)
Type in new name and press ENTER

EXPLANATION: Changes a file's name. Useful if you desire to provide a document with a more descriptive filename.

▶ Repetition Counter

see ESCAPE

▶ Replace

KEY SEQUENCE:
REPLACE (ALT + F2) key
Y or N for confirmation option
Type in Search string
ESC or →SEARCH (F2) or REPLACE (ALT + F2)
Type in Replace string
ESC or →SEARCH (F2) or REPLACE (ALT + F2)

EXPLANATION: Replaces a word, code, or phrase (Search string) with another word, code, or phrase (Replace string), beginning at the current cursor position and continuing to the end of the document. If you select the confirmation option, the program stops to ask for confirmation before replacing a Search string. If the string in the text is capitalized, the Replace string will also be capitalized.

You can perform the Replace on only a portion of a document by blocking text with the BLOCK

(ALT + F4) key before pressing REPLACE.

Version 4.2 users can press HOME before pressing the REPLACE (ALT + F2) key to extend the Replace command into headers, footers, footnotes, and endnotes.

▶ Retrieve a File From Disk

BY TYPING THE FILENAME

KEY SEQUENCE:
RETRIEVE (SHIFT + F10) key
Type in filename and press ENTER

EXPLANATION: Retrieves a copy of a file from disk onto the Typing screen for review, editing, or printing. Be sure to enter the name of a path (drive/directory) before the filename if the file is stored in other than the default drive. If the file is locked, WordPerfect requests a password.

FROM A LIST OF FILES

KEY SEQUENCE:
LIST FILES (F5) key
Type in name of drive/directory and press ENTER
Position cursor on a filename
1 (Retrieve)

97

EXPLANATION: Retrieves a copy of a file from disk onto the Typing screen for review, editing, or printing. If the file is locked, WordPerfect requests a password.

▶ Returns

HARD

KEY SEQUENCE:
ENTER

EXPLANATION: Moves the cursor down to the next line of text. Useful to end a short line of text, end a paragraph, or insert a blank line.

CODE INSERTED:
[HRt]

SOFT

KEY SEQUENCE:
None (performed by WordPerfect)

EXPLANATION: Starts the cursor at the beginning of the next line after you type a full line of text. This is known as "word wrap." The line end will readjust if text is later edited.

CODE INSERTED:
  [SRt]

Reveal Codes

KEY SEQUENCE:
  REVEAL CODES (ALT + F3) key

EXPLANATION: Splits the screen in half. The top window shows the text as if on the Typing screen. The bottom window shows the same text along with the location codes in that text. The two windows are separated by a ruler line. Useful to reveal codes when you wish to determine whether a feature which only takes effect at the printer has been activated or to find the location of a code you wish to delete.

Rewrite Screen

KEY SEQUENCE:
  SCREEN (CTRL + F3) key
  0 (Rewrite) or ENTER

EXPLANATION: Rewrites the document to ensure that text fits within the specified margins and that other format changes take effect. Useful if you turned Auto-Rewrite off (see AUTO-REWRITE) and now wish to update the text.

▶ Ruler Line

KEY SEQUENCE:
SCREEN (CTRL + F3) key
1 (Window)
↑ and ENTER

EXPLANATION: Reduces the Typing screen's window by one line and shows a ruler line displaying current margin and tab locations. To delete the ruler line, repeat the key sequence but press ↓ and ENTER or enter the number of lines as 0 when WordPerfect prompts for the number of lines in the window.

▶ Rush a Print Job

see CONTROL PRINT JOBS

▶ Save

BLOCK

KEY SEQUENCE:
BLOCK (ALT + F4) key
SAVE (F10) key
Type in filename and press ENTER

EXPLANATION: Stores a copy of the highlighted text into a file of its own. Useful if you wish to store just a part of a document on disk. If a file by that name already exists on disk, WordPerfect asks for confirmation to replace the old version with the new, screen version.

FILE (AND RETAIN DOCUMENT ON SCREEN)

KEY SEQUENCE:
SAVE (F10) key
Type in filename and press ENTER

EXPLANATION: Stores a copy of the screen version of the document on disk. If a file by that name already exists on disk, WordPerfect asks for confirmation to replace the old version with the new, screen version. The document remains on screen after being saved.

FILE (AND CLEAR SCREEN)

KEY SEQUENCE:
EXIT (F7) key
Y to save document
Type in filename and press ENTER
Y to exit WordPerfect or N to clear screen but remain
 in WordPerfect

EXPLANATION: Stores a copy of the screen version of the document on disk. If a file by that name already exists on disk, WordPerfect asks for confirmation to replace the old version with the new, screen version. After being saved, the document is cleared from the screen (unless you press CANCEL).

IN DOS TEXT FILE FORMAT

see DOS (ASCII) TEXT FILES

IN GENERIC WORD PROCESSING FORMAT (Version 4.2)

KEY SEQUENCE:
TEXT IN/OUT (CTRL + F5)
6 (Save in generic format)

EXPLANATION: Stores a file from the screen to disk in a generic word processing format. The format of the document is maintained, though it is stripped of WordPerfect codes.

IN WORDPERFECT (Version 4.1)

KEY SEQUENCE:
TEXT IN/OUT (CTRL + F5)
7 (Save in WordPerfect 4.1 format)

EXPLANATION: For Version 4.2 users, stores a file from the screen to disk in Version 4.1 format, so that in can be retrieved into WordPerfect Version 4.1.

▶ Search

KEY SEQUENCE (Forward):
→SEARCH (F2) key
Type in Search string
ESC or →SEARCH (F2)

KEY SEQUENCE (Reverse):
←SEARCH (SHIFT + F2) key
Type in Search string
ESC or →SEARCH (F2)

EXPLANATION: Positions the cursor just past the next occurrence of the Search string (word, code, or phrase) in the text. The Forward Search checks forward in the text for the next occurrence, while the Reverse Search checks backward only. Lowercase matches both lowercase and UPPERCASE letters, while UPPERCASE in a string matches only UPPERCASE letters.

You can perform the search on only a portion of a document by blocking text with the BLOCK (ALT + F4) key before pressing →SEARCH or ←-SEARCH.

Version 4.2 users can extend the Search command into headers, footers, footnotes, and endnotes by pressing HOME before pressing the →SEARCH (F2) key or the ←SEARCH (SHIFT + F2) key.

Select Lines, Paragraphs, Records

see SORT LINES, PARAGRAPHS, RECORDS

Select Print Options

see PRINT OPTIONS

Select Printers

see PRINTERS, SELECT

Sheet Feeder Bin Number

KEY SEQUENCE:
PRINT FORMAT (CTRL + F8) key
9 (Sheet Feeder Bin Number)

EXPLANATION: The default is bin 1. Changes the bin from which paper is fed into the printer (if you have defined your printer with a sheet feeder and more than one bin). Version 4.2 users can define up to 7 bins; version 4.1 users up to 3 bins.

CODE INSERTED:
  [Bin#:n]
  n = bin number

▷ **Shell**

see DOS, EXIT TO

▷ **Sort Lines, Paragraphs, Records**

BLOCK

KEY SEQUENCE:
  BLOCK (ALT + F4) key
  MERGE/SORT (CTRL + F9) key

EXPLANATION: Sorts a block of text currently on screen, whether lines, paragraphs or secondary merge records, into alphabetical or numeric order based on a specific word or field.

Selects records that meet a particular selection statement. Or performs both a sort and selection.

The default is to sort the block line by line in ascending order (A to Z or smallest number to largest number), based on the first word or numeral in each line. Press 1 (Perform Action), to begin the sort. Or change the Sort defaults as described below.

105

ENTIRE DOCUMENT

KEY SEQUENCE:
MERGE/SORT (CTRL + F9) key

ENTER or type in name of input file and press ENTER
   (if document is not on screen)

ENTER or type in name of output file and press
   ENTER (if you want the results placed on disk)

EXPLANATION: Sorts an entire document; the
document can be on screen or in a file on disk. You
can sort lines, paragraphs or secondary merge
files into alphabetical or numeric order based on a
specific word or field.

    Selects records that meet a particular selection
statement. Or performs both a sort and selection.

    The default is to sort line by line in ascending
order (A to Z or smallest number to largest
number), based on the first word or numeral in
each line. Press 1 (Perform Action), to begin the
sort. Or change the sort defaults as follows on the
Sort menu:

Action: Specify a Sort only, Select only, or both.
(Can only indicate a Select after having defined a
selection statement)

Keys: Specify the words and fields that will be
used to sort on or in the selection statement

Order: Specify ascending, which is A to Z or smallest to largest number, or descending, which is Z to A and largest to smallest.

Select: Specify a selection statement, the criteria on which text will be extracted, based on the defined keys.

Type: Specify whether to sort lines, paragraphs, or a secondary merge file.

View: Cursor moves up to the text about to be sorted, enabling you to move around in the text

When you change any of the Sort/Select defaults, they are altered until you change them again or until you exit WordPerfect.

Sorting Sequence

KEY SEQUENCE:
MERGE/SORT (CTRL + F9) key
3 (Sorting Sequence)

EXPLANATION: Alters the order in which text is sorted for text which uses the Scandinavian languages.

▶ Spacing, Line

see LINE SPACING

▶ Space, Hard

see HARD SPACE

▶ Special Characters

see CTRL/ALT KEY ASSIGNMENTS

▶ Speller

KEY SEQUENCE:
SPELL (CTRL + F2) key

EXPLANATION: Can spell check a word, page, or whole document; simply choose from the Spell menu. You can also spell check a portion of the document by blocking text with the BLOCK (ALT + F4) key before pressing SPELL.

The Speller function also allows you to change the supplemental dictionary used for the spell check, look up a word in the dictionary, or perform a word count (See WORD COUNT).

When WordPerfect highlights a word not found in the dictionary, you have six options to choose from:

108

Add word: Add the highlighted word to the supplemental dictionary.

Edit: Correct the highlighted word using the standard editing keys.

Look up: List additional words based on a word pattern.

Phonetic: List additional words based on how the highlighted word sounds.

Skip: Ignore the highlighted word for the rest of the spell check.

Skip once: Ignore this one occurrence of the highlighted word.

You can also spell check only a portion of the document by blocking text with the BLOCK (ALT+F4) key before pressing SPELL.

Split Screen

see WINDOWS

Startup (Slash) Options

EXPLANATION: Loads WordPerfect and activates one or more special options at the same time.

Rather than typing WP to load WordPerfect, type one of the following:

WP/B-minutes: Sets up the Timed Backup feature, whereby WordPerfect backs up the document on screen to a temporary file at the minute-interval specified. This protects against losing large amounts of text in the event of a power failure.

WP/D-d: Redirects WordPerfect's temporary files to another drive, where d: is the drive (such as B:).

WP filename: Retrieves the file specified as soon as WordPerfect is loaded.

WP/I: Used if you have a hard disk system but are loading WordPerfect from a floppy or if you install WordPerfect from a copy.

WP/M-macroname: Executes the macro specified as soon as WordPerfect is loaded.

WP/NF: Activates the nonflash option in the event that your screen periodically goes blank or you use a windowing program.

WP/NS: Activates the nonsync option to help certain computers from hanging.

WP/R: Speeds up operations of the WordPerfect program. Use only if your computer is equipped with at least 384K of RAM Memory.

WP/S: Displays the Set-up menu as soon as WordPerfect is loaded. From this menu, you can permanently alter the defaults for settings such as margins, tabs, page length, footnotes, and paragraph numbering. In addition, the Set-up menu enables you to do the following:

- indicate the location of the dictionary and the-saurus files (if not in the same location as the WordPerfect program file)

- change screen and beep defaults

- set the timed backup or original backup options.

Stop Printing

see CONTROL PRINT JOBS

Strikeout

KEY SEQUENCE:
BLOCK (ALT + F4) key to highlight text
MARK TEXT (ALT + F5) key
4 (Strikeout)

EXPLANATION: Marks text for deletion. Useful when you wish to mark characters of text that could possibly be deleted, without actually deleting the text. When the document is printed, a dash (or other character) appears where the text is marked for deletion. (See also REMOVE RED-LINE AND STRIKEOUT)

CODE INSERTED:
[StrkOut] preceding the text
[s] following the text

Summaries

see DOCUMENT COMMENTS AND
SUMMARIES

Super/Subscript

KEY SEQUENCE:
SUPER/SUBSCRIPT (SHIFT + F1) key
1 (Superscript) or 2 (Subscript)
Type character

EXPLANATION: Directs the printer to position the next character typed approximately one-third line up (superscript) or down (subscript). Useful in equations and other statistical typing.

The text on screen is not affected, but the line indicator (Ln) on the status line indicates the line on which the text will be printed. In addition, an "S" appears on the status line before you type a superscripted character, and an "s" appears before you type a subscripted character.

To super or subscript more than one character at a time, block the group of characters with the BLOCK (ALT + F4) key before pressing SUPER/SUBSCRIPT.

CODE INSERTED:
[SuprScrpt] or [SubScrpt] in front of each character

▷ Suppress Formatting for Current Page

KEY SEQUENCE:
PAGE FORMAT (ALT + F8) key
8 (Suppress)

EXPLANATION: Suppresses page numbering, headers, or footers for the current page, depending on which of 8 options you choose. Useful for the first page of a letter or report.

CODE INSERTED:
[Suppress:n]
n = format option chosen

▶ Switch Windows

see WINDOWS

▶ Tabs

SET

KEY SEQUENCE (Version 4.2):
LINE FORMAT (SHIFT + F8) key
1 or 2 (Tabs)

KEY SEQUENCE (Version 4.1):
LINE FORMAT (SHIFT + F8) key
1 (Tabs for positions 0 through 159)
or
2 (Extended tabs for positions 160 to 250)

EXPLANATION: The tab ruler indicates the current tab stop settings. The default is every 5 spaces up to position 160, and every 10 spaces from 160 to 250. To erase the current tab stops from the cursor to the end of the tab ruler line, press DELETE EOL (CTRL + END). To delete one tab stop, position the cursor and press DEL. To set evenly-spaced tab stops, type the starting position, a comma, and the number of spaces between tabs (for example 15,5). To set one tab stop, position the cursor and press TAB.

114

Version 4.2 users can set 7 different tab stop styles: left, left with a dot leader, right, right with a dot leader, decimal, decimal with a dot leader, or center. Type L, R, C, or D respectively at a tab location. For a dot leader, then type a period. (Pressing TAB inserts a left tab.)

Version 4.1 users can set only 1 tab stop style: left (but can create the same formats using the Center or Tab Align features).

CODE INSERTED:
[Tab Set:n,n,n,...]
n = tab stop location

USE

KEY SEQUENCE:
TAB

EXPLANATION: Positions the cursor at the next tab stop. All text typed on that tab stop to the end of that line is aligned flush left (unless, in version 4.2, another tab stop style was set for that tab stop.) Other features that work on tab stops include Center, →Indent, →Indent←, ←Margin Release and Tab Align.

CODE INSERTED:
[TAB]

▶ Tab Align

USE

KEY SEQUENCE:
TAB ALIGN (CTRL + F6)

EXPLANATION: Lines up text or numbers over a
tab stop on the alignment character, such as on
the decimal so that a column of numbers is
aligned on the decimal point.

CODE INSERTED:
[A] preceding the first character of the entry
[a] preceding the alignment character

SET ALIGNMENT CHARACTER

KEY SEQUENCE:
LINE FORMAT (SHIFT + F8) key
6 (Align Char)

EXPLANATION: Changes the character used to
align text or numbers on a tab stop. The default
alignment character is the decimal point (period).
When WordPerfect prompts "Align Char = .",
type in the new alignment character.

CODE INSERTED:
[Align Char:n]
n = character

▷ Tab Ruler

see RULER LINE

▷ Tables of Authorities (Version 4.2)

DEFINE

KEY SEQUENCE:
MARK TEXT (ALT + F5) key
6 (Other Options)
4 (Define Table of Authorities)
Type section number
Select style options

EXPLANATION: Defines the location and style options of the table of authorities (citations) for when it is generated. Style options include the following:

- whether page numbers are preceded by dot leaders (option 1)

- whether underlining is allowed (option 2)

- whether blank lines should be inserted between authorities (option 3)

You must create a defintion for each section in the table of authorities.

CODE INSERTED:
 [DefMark:ToA,n]
 n = section number

EDIT

KEY SEQUENCE:
 MARK TEXT (ALT + F5) key
 6 (other options)
 7 (Edit Table of Authorities Full Form)
 Edit the text
 EXIT (F7)
 Type section number and press ENTER

EXPLANATION: Edits the full form of an authority after the authority has already been marked.

GENERATE

see GENERATE INDEXES, LISTS, TABLES

MARK TEXT FOR

KEY SEQUENCE (Full Form):
 BLOCK TEXT (ALT + F4) key
 MARK TEXT (ALT + F5) key
 6 (ToA)
 Type section number and press ENTER
 Edit the authority
 EXIT (F7) key
 Type in short form and press ENTER

KEY SEQUENCE (Short Form):
MARK TEXT (ALT + F5) key
4 (Short Form)
Type in short from and press ENTER

EXPLANATION: Marks the word or phrase you wish to be included in a table of contents when generated. A full form is used the first time you mark an authority; a short form is used as a nickname to reference the full form.

CODE INSERTED:
[ToA:n;t,<full form>] or [ToA:;t]
n = section number
t = text of short form

▶ Tables of Contents

DEFINE

KEY SEQUENCE (Version 4.2):
MARK TEXT (ALT + F5) key
6 (Other Options)
2 (Define Table of Contents)
Type number of levels
Indicate if last level is to be wrapped
Select a numbering style

KEY SEQUENCE (Version 4.1):
MARK TEXT (ALT + F5) key
6 (Define)
6 (Table of Contents)
Type the number of levels
Indicate if last level is to be wrapped
Select a numbering style

EXPLANATION: Defines the location and page numbering style of the table of contents for when it is generated.

CODE INSERTED:
[DefMark:ToC,n]
n = number of levels

GENERATE

see GENERATE INDEXES, LISTS, TABLES

MARK TEXT FOR

KEY SEQUENCE:
BLOCK TEXT (ALT + F4) key
MARK TEXT (ALT + F5) key
1 (ToC)
Type table of contents level

EXPLANATION: Marks the word or phrase you wish to be included in a table of contents when generated.

CODE INSERTED:
  [Mark:ToC,n]
  n = table of contents level

▷ Text Columns

see COLUMNS OF TEXT

▷ Text Lines (Number of Single Spaced)

see PAGE LENGTH

▷ Thesaurus

KEY SEQUENCE:
  THESAURUS (ALT + F1) key

EXPLANATION: Provides synonyms for the high-lighted word where the cursor is located (Version 4.2 also includes antonyms). Use the arrow keys to move the cursor within the list of synonyms/antonyms. The following options are available on the Thesaurus menu:

Clear column: Clear the list of synonyms/antonyms for the last word selected.

Look up word: Look up synonyms/antonyms for another word.

Replace word: Substitutes the word corresponding to the letter you select for the highlighted word.

View doc: Cursor moves up to the text, enabling you to move around in the text.

Time
see DATE (AND TIME)

Top Margin
see MARGINS

Transfer Files To/From WordPerfect
see CONVERT FILES TO/FROM WORDPERFECT, DOS (ASCII) TEXT FILES; and SAVE

▶ Typeover Mode

KEY SEQUENCE:
INS

EXPLANATION: Characters you type will replace existing characters. INS is a toggle, which switches between Insert and Typeover modes. The initial setting is Insert mode.

When in Typeover mode, the message "Typeover" appears on the status line.

▶ Type-Thru

KEY SEQUENCE:
PRINT (SHIFT + F7) key
5 (Type-thru)
1 (by line) or 2 (by character)

EXPLANATION: Makes the printer work like a typewriter. Characters you type are printed as soon as you type the ENTER key (Type-thru by line) or as soon as they are typed (Type-thru by character).Not all printers can support these features and some can support only Type-thru by line.

► Undelete (Undo)

KEY SEQUENCE:
CANCEL (F1) key
1 (Restore) or 2 (Show Previous Deletion)

EXPLANATION: If no menu or prompt is on the screen, recovers any of the last three deletion levels, where a deletion level is a group of consecutive deletions. The deletion level is shown in inverse video at the current cursor position.

► Underline

KEY SEQUENCE:
UNDERLINE (F8) key

EXPLANATION: Produces characters that are underlined when printed. On screen, the underlined text is actually underlined on monochrome monitors and shown in a different color on color monitors.

When typing text, the UNDERLINE key is a toggle switch; it turns Underline on if it was off, or vice versa. It can also be used to underline text that you have already typed if you first turn Block on and highlight the text to be underlined before pressing UNDERLINE.

CODE INSERTED:

[U] preceding the underlined text

[u] following the underlined text

> ## Underline Style

KEY SEQUENCE:

PRINT FORMAT (CTRL + F8) key

5 (Non-continuous Single)

or

6 (Non-continuous Double)

or

7 (Continuous Single)

or

8 (Continuous Double)

EXPLANATION: Determines how underlining will appear on the printed page. Choices are as follows:

- non-continuous, where tabs are not underlined

- continuous, where tabs are underlined

- single, where a single line is used as the underline character

- double, where a double line is used as the underline character

  Not all printers support double underlining.

CODE INSERTED:
[Undrl Style:n]
n = style option

▶ Widow/Orphan Protection

KEY SEQUENCE:
PAGE FORMAT (ALT + F8) key
A (Widow/Orphan)
Y to confirm

EXPLANATION: Ensures that the initial or final line of a paragraph is not stranded on a separate page due to a soft page break. With Widow/Orphan Protection on, a page break may occur one line early or one line late to keep the first or last line together with the rest of the paragraph.

CODE INSERTED:
[W/O On] or [W/O Off]

▶ Windows

SPLIT

KEY SEQUENCE:
SCREEN (CTRL + F3) key
1 (Window)
Type number of lines and press ENTER

EXPLANATION: Splits the screen into two windows, separated by a tab ruler (ruler line). The top window contains Doc 1, while the bottom window contains Doc 2. To return screen to one window, follow sequence above and enter the number of lines as 0 or as the full size of the screen (24 for a standard size monitor) when WordPerfect prompts for the number of lines in the window.

SWITCH

KEY SEQUENCE:
SWITCH (SHIFT + F3) key

EXPLANATION: Switches between the Doc 1 and Doc 2 windows. The status line indicates which document is on screen.

▶ Word Count

KEY SEQUENCE:
SPELL (CTRL + F2) key
6 (Count)

EXPLANATION: Counts the number of words in the document. It can also be used to count the words in a highlighted block of text if you first turn Block on, highlight the text to be counted, and then press SPELL.

► Word Search

KEY SEQUENCE:
LIST FILES (F5) key
Type in name of drive/directory and press ENTER
9 (Word Search)
Type in word pattern and press ENTER

EXPLANATION: On the List Files screen, lists those files containing the indicated word pattern. The word pattern can contain one or more words. For two words separated by a comma, WordPerfect searches for documents that contain either word. For two words separated by a space or semi-colon (;), WordPerfect searches for documents that contain both words. For words within quotation marks, WordPerfect searches for documents the contain that exact phrase. You can search through a specified number of files by marking the files you wish to search with an asterisk before pressing 9, Word Search (see also MARK FILES).